Original title:
Passion Pursuit

Author: Tim Wood
ISBN HARDBACK: 978-9916-88-044-9
ISBN PAPERBACK: 978-9916-88-045-6

Allure of the Unattainable

In shadows cast by dreams we chase,
Whispers linger, a fleeting grace.
Stars ignite the darkened sky,
Yet just beyond, they wander by.

The mountain peaks we yearn to climb,
Echoes of a distant rhyme.
A touch, a glance, forever missed,
In every chance, our hopes persist.

We write our tales on sands of time,
Each word a note, each phrase a rhyme.
Invisible threads pull us near,
Yet love's embrace remains unclear.

A wistful sigh at twilight's call,
The beauty in the rise and fall.
For in the chase, we find our way,
In longing's grasp, we choose to stay.

Horizons of the Heart

Beyond the dawn, where dreams align,
A landscape vast, a soul's design.
With every breath, new paths emerge,
In the embrace where passions surge.

The colors swirl, a vibrant blend,
A journey carved where love ascends.
Through valleys low and mountains high,
The heart will seek, the heart will fly.

Beneath the stars, our secrets shared,
In whispered words, our souls prepared.
Each horizon holds a promise bright,
Guiding us home through the night.

So hand in hand, we chase the light,
Two spirits soaring into the night.
With every step, we find our place,
In the horizon's warm embrace.

Unruly Sparks in the Quiet

In the stillness, whispers play,
Flickering dreams that sway.
Crimson embers dance with fate,
Unruly sparks never wait.

Silent echoes break the night,
Hidden tales take their flight.
Softly glowing, hearts ignite,
In quietude, they shine bright.

The Hunt for Life's Elixirs

Chasing shadows, we seek more,
Secrets behind every door.
Drops of joy, a fleeting taste,
Life's elixirs, never waste.

Rivers flow with hues untold,
In every heart, a spirit bold.
Sips of laughter, tears of grace,
In the hunt, we find our place.

Heartbeats in the Dark

In the twilight, pulses race,
Every thump a sacred space.
In the silence, truths unwind,
Heartbeats echo, intertwined.

Secrets whispered in the night,
Yearning souls embrace the light.
Finding solace, dreams embark,
Together, we dance in the dark.

Beneath the Veil of Want

Hidden desires in the night,
Whispering softly, out of sight.
Longing hearts beneath the glow,
A silent pact, we come to know.

In every glance, a world unseen,
Dreams intertwine where we have been.
Beneath the veil, we dance and weave,
In shadows deep, we learn to believe.

Captivated by the Unknown

A mystery calls from far away,
Curious hearts begin to sway.
Through winding paths, we seek the light,
Captivated by the unknown night.

Every chance leads us astray,
Yet in the dark, we wish to stay.
With every breath, the thrill of chase,
To find ourselves in time and space.

The Yearning Journey

Onward we travel, hearts ablaze,
Mapping out the winding ways.
Each step a dance, a brand new song,
The yearning journey, we've come along.

Through valleys low and mountains high,
With hope as wings, we learn to fly.
In every moment, joy and pain,
The lessons learned will not be vain.

Yearning Beyond the Horizon

In the twilight's soft embrace,
Dreams take flight like doves in space.
Whispers of the distant shore,
Echo in my heart, evermore.

Stars above, they gently gleam,
Guiding me through silent dreams.
Each wave sings a siren's song,
Pulling me where I belong.

With each step, the world unfolds,
Secrets whispered, tales retold.
The sun dips low, a golden sign,
Yearning stirs within, divine.

Across the vast and open sea,
I search for what is meant to be.
In the space 'twixt hope and fear,
The horizon calls me ever near.

In the Grip of Longing

Beneath the moon's soft silver glow,
A heart is heavy, aching slow.
Memories dance like shadows cast,
In the silence, echoes last.

Whispers linger on the breeze,
Carrying secrets through the trees.
Every star a wish unspun,
Longing lingers, never done.

Though time may heal the deepest pain,
The heart still yearns, a silent chain.
In dreams, a love I can't define,
In the grip of longing, I pine.

Days pass like clouds drifting high,
Underneath the vast, endless sky.
In the quiet, I find no end,
Longing's kiss, my constant friend.

The Call of Sacred Ambition

In the stillness of the night,
Ambitions spark with fierce delight.
Dreams ignite a fiery dance,
Whispers of a bold romance.

The mountains rise, a daunting sight,
Yet within me burns a light.
Steps I take on paths unknown,
With each heartbeat, courage grown.

Every challenge, like a stone,
Shapes my will, the seeds I've sown.
Voices of the past inspire,
Fueling my relentless fire.

The call to reach beyond the skies,
Is the echo of my cries.
With faith as my guiding star,
I venture forth, no dream too far.

Swept Away by Wild Winds

The tempest rages, fierce and bold,
As stories of the wild unfold.
With every gust, spirits soar,
Carried away to distant shores.

Clouds collide, a mighty roar,
Nature's fury, an open door.
Hearts entwined with every breeze,
Swept away with such sweet ease.

Beneath the darkened stormy skies,
We find our strength as thunder cries.
Together, facing what may come,
In wild winds, we are at home.

As daylight breaks and calm returns,
Hope ignites, my spirit yearns.
In the dance of nature's song,
I find a place where I belong.

Heart on Fire

In the silence, embers glow,
Whispers of love, soft and low.
Passions burn, igniting the night,
A flame of hope, a beacon bright.

With each heartbeat, sparks arise,
Promises held in longing sighs.
Through the darkness, we'll ignite,
Our hearts ablaze, a shared light.

Fires entwined, forever soar,
Together we dance, forevermore.
No shadows cast can dim this glow,
With hearts on fire, we’ll always know.

Unyielding Desires

In the depths where shadows dwell,
Yearnings rise, casting a spell.
Dreams entwined, a fervent chase,
Unyielding desires we embrace.

Through the storms and skies of gray,
We forge our path, come what may.
With every breath, we seek the flame,
In hearts united, we remain the same.

A whisper calls, a tender plea,
In passion's grip, we are set free.
With every moment, let love steer,
In unyielding desires, we persevere.

The Dance of Devotion

With subtle steps, our souls entwine,
In rhythm strong, your heart in mine.
Each glance ignites a timeless tune,
A melody beneath the moon.

Through swirling winds and gentle grace,
The dance unfolds in warm embrace.
With every twirl, we spin the night,
Our devotion shines, a pure delight.

In silent moments, we hold tight,
Two beating hearts, a guiding light.
As shadows fade and dawn breaks clear,
In the dance of love, I keep you near.

Embracing the Flame

In the warmth of a glowing night,
We gather close, hearts held tight.
With every spark, our fears dissolve,
In this fire, our dreams evolve.

A flicker bright, our spirits rise,
Within our hearts, a sweet surprise.
In passion's glow, we find the way,
Embracing the flame, come what may.

With hands entwined, we face the storm,
In each other's arms, we feel warm.
Together we'll kindle the light,
Embracing the flame, hearts in flight.

Fanning the Flames

In the dark where embers glow,
Whispers rise and shadows flow.
A spark ignites the night so still,
Fanning flames with passion's thrill.

Hearts ablaze in the quiet hour,
Drawing strength from passion’s power.
Every flicker tells a tale,
Of love’s tempestuous gale.

With every breath, let the fire grow,
Consuming fears that come and go.
Together we will stoke the heat,
In the dance where two hearts meet.

So let us shine, both fierce and bright,
In the warmth of love’s soft light.
Fanning flames with gentle grace,
Creating a haven, our sacred space.

Dancing Between Stars

In the night where dreams take flight,
We twirl beneath the silver light.
Galaxies whisper secrets old,
As stardust dreams begin to unfold.

Steps we trace in cosmic glow,
Waltzing where the comets flow.
Each movement soft, a timeless art,
Uniting souls, two worlds apart.

The universe sings a tranquil tune,
Beneath the watchful eyes of the moon.
In this realm where magic sways,
We dance between the starlit rays.

With every breath, the cosmos hums,
A rhythm sweet, as adventure comes.
In the embrace of twilight's bar,
We find our place, dancing between stars.

The Allure of Adventure

Wanderlust calls with a soft refrain,
An open road and the promise of gain.
Mountains rise and rivers flow,
To distant lands we yearn to go.

With hearts unbound, we chase the sun,
Every journey, a race to run.
The thrill of the unknown awaits,
Where destiny and fate creates.

Every path is etched in time,
A tapestry of tales, sublime.
From valleys deep to skies so wide,
Adventure pulses, our trusted guide.

So let us roam where wild winds blow,
With courage strong, hearts aglow.
For in the chase of life's sweet call,
We find ourselves, we find it all.

Restless Hearts

Beneath the moon, our shadows play,
Restless hearts fight night and day.
In silent whispers, dreams take flight,
Chasing wishes hidden from sight.

Through winding paths and tangled trees,
We seek the truth, a gentle breeze.
The fire within can’t be contained,
In love's embrace, we remain unchained.

Fate may toil, and time may bend,
But restless hearts will not pretend.
Each pulse a note in life’s refrain,
Together we dance through joy and pain.

So let us wander, hand in hand,
Building castles in the sand.
For in every tear and every smile,
Our restless hearts will go the mile.

In Pursuit of Bliss

In the dawn's gentle light,
Dreams awaken and take flight.
With hope as our guiding star,
We chase the joy that's never far.

Through fields of laughter, we roam,
Finding solace far from home.
With every step, our hearts ignite,
In pursuit of bliss, we find our light.

Moments cherished, memories made,
The price of love, we gladly paid.
With open arms, we embrace the day,
In the rhythm of life, we sway.

In every heartbeat, a whisper calls,
Through valleys deep and mountain halls.
Together we strive, together we rise,
In pursuit of bliss, beneath the skies.

The Melody of Ambition

A tune that lingers in the air,
Drives us forward without a care.
With each note, our spirits soar,
The melody of ambition we adore.

In the silence, dreams take shape,
We weave our lives, no chance to escape.
A symphony of hopes and fears,
In the harmony, we shed our tears.

With passion ignited, we press on,
Each setback fades with the dawn.
For in the pursuit of our grand design,
The melody of ambition shines.

Together we rise, together we stand,
Holding tight to one another's hand.
As we journey through the ebb and flow,
In the melody of ambition, we grow.

Rhapsody of Desire

In the whispers of the night,
Desires dance in soft moonlight.
With every glance, a world ignites,
A rhapsody of heart's delights.

Through the shadows, secrets bloom,
In passion's embrace, we find our room.
Each heartbeat sings a timeless song,
In the rhapsody where we belong.

With fervent dreams and unspoken lies,
We chase the stars that fill the skies.
In every moment, passion's fire,
Ignites the rhapsody of desire.

Together we chase what we cannot see,
In the depths of longing, we are free.
With open hearts, we dare to aspire,
In the rhapsody of our burning desire.

The Spark Within

A flicker deep inside the soul,
A fire that whispers, 'You are whole.'
In trials faced, the light will show,
The spark within begins to glow.

Through darkness cast, we find our way,
With every dawn, a brand new day.
Together we nurture this sacred flame,
The spark within, it knows our name.

In unity and strength, we stand,
With faith as our guide, and love so grand.
With hearts ablaze and spirits bright,
The spark within ignites the night.

Through life's vast journey, we shall shine,
With every moment, a gift divine.
Embrace the warmth, let it begin,
For greatness lies in the spark within.

The Heartbeat of Aspiration

In the quiet whispers of the night,
Dreams take flight, a hopeful sight.
With every pulse, a fire burns,
The heartache teaches, the spirit learns.

Reaching high on peaks untold,
With courage gathered, battle bold.
Each step forward, a seed to sow,
In fields of passion, watch it grow.

Through shadows deep and valleys wide,
A light ignites, a truth inside.
With every heartbeat, a call to rise,
Embrace the journey, touch the skies.

The echo of ambition sings,
Carried forth on daring wings.
For in this life, what we chase,
Is the heartbeat of our grace.

Living for the Thrill

Chasing moments, wild and free,
Each heartbeat echoes, 'come with me.'
Racing winds, the pulse of life,
In every heartbeat, joy and strife.

Beneath the stars, we laugh and spin,
Embracing chaos, letting in.
From mountain heights to ocean waves,
The thrill of living, what it gave.

With every breath, the world unfolds,
Adventures waiting, tales untold.
In fleeting seconds, we believe,
That life's true thrill is to achieve.

So dance through storms, embrace the fire,
Feel the rush of pure desire.
For in each heartbeat, feel it still,
The vibrant joy of living thrill.

The Ecstasy of Chasing Light

In every dawn, a story starts,
With rays that kiss and warm our hearts.
Through golden hues, our spirits rise,
Chasing light beneath vast skies.

With gentle whispers, shadows flee,
In vibrant colors, we are free.
Each glimmer dances, each sparkle sings,
The ecstasy that daylight brings.

Through valleys dark, we'll find our way,
In quest for hope, come what may.
When twilight falls and stars ignite,
We'll chase the dream of endless light.

For in this journey, hand in hand,
The ecstasy, a promised land.
Together we'll shine, forever bright,
In the bliss of chasing light.

Surrender to the Journey

With every step, the path unfolds,
A story written, life retold.
In quiet moments, we must yield,
To the journey, our hearts are sealed.

Through winding roads and gentle streams,
We find our strength in whispered dreams.
In every stumble, grace will find,
The courage nestled within the mind.

Let go the fear that holds us fast,
In surrender, freedom's cast.
Every heartbeat leads the way,
Through the night and into day.

For life's a dance, a winding song,
To surrender is where we belong.
In each embrace, the world will see,
The beauty found in letting be.

Embers in the Night

Flickering softly, shadows play,
Echoes of warmth in fading gray.
A dance of memories, dreams take flight,
Hope ignites within the night.

Stars in silence, watch the glow,
A whispering breeze begins to flow.
Each spark a story, softly told,
In the dark, our hearts unfold.

Through the stillness, secrets weave,
Leaving behind what we believe.
Among the ashes, we find our way,
A path illuminated, come what may.

Embers flicker, moments last,
In the night, we hold the past.
With every breath, we feel alive,
In the darkness, our souls thrive.

Chasing Dreams Beneath the Stars

Under the vast and endless sky,
We lift our hopes, we learn to fly.
A journey starts with whispered wishes,
To reach the shores of hidden riches.

Footprints soft on the silver sand,
Guided by starlight, hand in hand.
Each dream a beacon, shining bright,
Leading us deeper into the night.

Through valleys deep and mountains high,
We chase the dreams that never die.
With every step, the future glows,
A tapestry of where love flows.

United hearts feel the thrill,
With every challenge, we grow still.
Beneath the stars, we find our way,
In the night, we learn to sway.

The Fire that Ignites

In the hearth, a flame does dance,
With every flicker, we take a chance.
Memories kindled, stories shared,
In this fire, we are bared.

The glow reflects in earnest eyes,
A bond ignited, no goodbyes.
With every spark, passion swells,
In the warmth, true love dwells.

Crackling softly, the wood does sing,
A melody of the hope we bring.
Through the shadows, our spirits rise,
In the fire, we find our ties.

As night descends, the flames anew,
Our hearts ablaze with love so true.
In the stillness, we embrace,
The fire that ignites, our sacred space.

Whispers of an Unquenchable Flame

In the silence, a heart beats loud,
A whisper floats beneath the cloud.
A flame that flickers, never burns out,
In the shadows, we dance about.

Through the days, we chase the light,
With every spark, we ignite the night.
Voices weave like threads of gold,
Stories of love and dreams retold.

Unquenchable fire in the soul,
A warmth that makes the spirit whole.
In every sigh and every glance,
We rekindle our sacred dance.

Together we rise, together we fall,
An everlasting bond that conquers all.
In the whispers, our hearts proclaim,
This love, a never-ending flame.

Whispers of Longing

In the silence, shadows play,
Dreams of you drift far away.
Softly calling, echoes sigh,
In the night, my heart does cry.

Stars above, they watch and wait,
Yearning souls, we tempt our fate.
In the twilight, secrets blend,
Longing for a love to mend.

Time stands still while hearts embrace,
In the dark, I seek your face.
Every heartbeat, every glance,
Pulls me deep into this dance.

Whispers linger in the air,
Tangled thoughts beyond compare.
Feelings bloom, like flowers bright,
In our hearts, a shared delight.

The Journey of Hearts

Two souls wander through the night,
Chasing dreams, embracing light.
Hand in hand, we face the dawn,
With each step, together drawn.

Mountains high and valleys low,
Through the storms, our love will grow.
Every trial we will withstand,
Side by side, we'll make our stand.

Whispers guide us on our way,
In the dark, we find our day.
In your eyes, I see the truth,
A timeless bond, our tender youth.

With each moment, we explore,
Hearts entwined, we seek for more.
In the journey, love will lead,
Together, we fulfill the need.

Ecstasy in Motion

Feel the rhythm, hearts align,
Every heartbeat, pure divine.
In the moment, passions blaze,
Lost in time, a fervent haze.

Dance with me under the stars,
Feel the pulse from Mars to bars.
Every touch ignites the fire,
In your arms, my soul's desire.

Spinning worlds in endless chase,
In your gaze, I find my place.
Whirling dreams, our bodies sway,
In this dance, we drift away.

Here and now, let moments gleam,
In this ecstasy, we dream.
Feel the music, let it play,
As we lose ourselves today.

Boundless Yearnings

A horizon we can’t ignore,
Longing hearts that yearn for more.
In the night, our spirits soar,
Boundless dreams on distant shore.

Waves of passion crash and flow,
In the stillness, feelings grow.
Every sigh a soft embrace,
In your love, I find my place.

Chasing shadows, hearts entwined,
Seeking solace, love defined.
With each sunset, colors blend,
In this journey, we transcend.

Boundless yearnings, never end,
On this path, our hearts depend.
In the fabric of the night,
We are woven, pure delight.

The Intensity of the Chase

In shadows deep, we make our flight,
With every heartbeat, a spark ignites.
Whispers echo in the night air,
The pulse of passion, a thrilling snare.

Chasing glimmers of fleeting light,
Through tangled paths, our souls unite.
With every turn, there's more to learn,
In this wild dance, for which we yearn.

Steps align on this vibrant trail,
Fainting footsteps tell our tale.
In the fervor, we push and race,
Lost in the intensity of the chase.

But as dawn breaks, we pause and see,
The essence of love is wild and free.
In every moment, our spirits soar,
An endless pursuit, forever more.

Impressions of the Heart

In a silent glance, worlds collide,
With unspoken words, love will guide.
Every heartbeat, a gentle brush,
Creating a canvas, soft as hush.

Fleeting moments paint our days,
In vibrant hues, through swirling ways.
Tender echoes, souls entwined,
Each impression, a treasure defined.

Strokes of laughter, shadows of tears,
In the gallery of hopes and fears.
Every sigh, a brush of fate,
Where love's sweet whispers reverberate.

Memories linger, vivid and true,
With every heartbeat, I feel you.
In this portrait, hearts will dance,
An art of love, a timeless romance.

Between Desires and Dreams

In the space where wishes dwell,
Between desires, we weave our spell.
Tender hopes hover like mist,
Each moment begs to be kissed.

A tug of war in the night's embrace,
Dreams chase shadows, a fleeting race.
Yearning souls in soft twilight,
Balance the dark with the light.

In whispers shared beneath the stars,
We navigate our hidden scars.
With every step towards the aim,
In this dance, we play the game.

Between the lines of heart and mind,
We seek the paths that fate designed.
In this liminal space, we soar,
Between desires and dreams, evermore.

The Expedition of Eagerness

With unyielding hearts, we set to roam,
In the wild woods, we search for home.
Each rustling leaf, a call to adventure,
In eagerness, we find our center.

Through valleys deep and mountains high,
Together we laugh, together we sigh.
Moments unfold like maps in hand,
In every step, we understand.

The sunrises glow with colors bright,
Fueling our passion, igniting the night.
With every dawn, new dreams we chase,
In this expedition, we've found our place.

No matter the trials that lie ahead,
In eagerness, we are gently led.
With open hearts, we journey far,
Together, destined to be our own star.

In the Shadow of Dreams

In the quiet whispers, secrets lie,
Beneath the moon's glow, wishes fly.
Silhouettes dancing on the edge of night,
Chasing the visions that feel so right.

Echoes of laughter in the still air,
Fleeting moments, a tender care.
Each shadow cast tells a story deep,
In the realm of dreams, our hearts will leap.

Waves of silence, a gentle sigh,
Time stands still, as dreams pass by.
In the twilight glow, we find our way,
In the shadow of dreams, we long to stay.

Fates intertwine, like stars aligned,
Each thread a journey, uniquely bind.
In the darkness, our hopes ignite,
In the shadow of dreams, we take flight.

Journey to the Heart's Desire

Across the hills, the road unfolds,
With every step, a tale is told.
Whispers of passion in the breeze,
Guiding us forth, putting minds at ease.

Mountains high and rivers wide,
Within our hearts, we carry pride.
Through valleys deep, we seek the light,
On this journey, our souls take flight.

Time may bend, and paths may stray,
Yet hope remains, a bright array.
With every heartbeat, we draw near,
Journeying forth to what we hold dear.

In the embrace of the unknown,
Together we walk, never alone.
With dreams ablaze, we dive and soar,
A journey to the heart, forevermore.

The Art of Compulsion

A dance of shadows, a flicker of need,
Compelled by whispers, hearts take heed.
In the grip of desire, we lose our way,
The art of compulsion holds sway.

Fingertips tracing the lines of fate,
Each choice a dance, both love and hate.
The fire within burns fierce and bright,
In the art of compulsion, we find our light.

Caught in a web of enchanting dreams,
Life pulls us under, or so it seems.
Through chaos and clarity, we will tread,
In the art of compulsion, we forge ahead.

With every heartbeat, a silent plea,
Chasing the shadows that long to be free.
In the tapestry woven of longing's thread,
The art of compulsion, it’s where we’re led.

With Every Breath, I Yearn

With every breath, a story unfolds,
Whispers of longing, secrets untold.
In the silence, my heart can speak,
A gentle reminder of all I seek.

Through the ticking clock, time drifts by,
Moments linger, like dreams that fly.
With every sigh, a wish takes flight,
In the quiet depths of the night.

Stars shimmer softly in the vast expanse,
Each twinkle a promise, a chance to dance.
With every heartbeat, my spirit's call,
I yearn for the beauty that encompasses all.

In the rustling leaves and the softest breeze,
In every longing, a chance to seize.
With every breath, I find my way,
Yearning for love, come what may.

The Allure of Daring Horizons

Beyond the edge where shadows play,
The sky blushes in twilight's sway.
With hearts ablaze, we chase the light,
To find our dreams beyond the night.

Each whisper hints of paths untold,
Silent stories in colors bold.
With every step, the unknown calls,
We rise, we soar, we heed its thralls.

The horizon stretches, wide and vast,
In its embrace, our fears are cast.
Adventure waits, so sweet, so near,
To brave the depths of what we fear.

With every breath, we break the mold,
The allure of daring dreams unfolds.
In this pursuit, we find our grace,
A journey shared, a timeless space.

Mosaic of a Thousand Wishes

In vibrant hues the dreams collide,
A tapestry where hopes reside.
Each fragment holds a whispered prayer,
A wish released into the air.

Collect the pieces, bright and rare,
From distant lands, from everywhere.
They weave a tale of love and strife,
The mosaic of our inner life.

With every thought, a shape appears,
Reflecting laughter, echoing tears.
Colors blend in a dance so free,
A masterpiece of you and me.

The wishes shine, a guiding light,
In darkest hours, they burn so bright.
Together we'll craft, with heart and hand,
A world enchanted, a wishful land.

Seeking the Undefined

In shadows cast by dreams unseen,
We wander where the void has been.
Each step unveils a brand new quest,
To seek the things that manifest.

The lines we draw are blurred with time,
In spaces void of reasoned rhyme.
Exploring depths where few have tread,
We dance on thoughts that dance instead.

With open hearts, we navigate,
The undefined, we contemplate.
In every question, answers lie,
So bold we leap; we dare to fly.

The journey twists, unfolds anew,
A path of stars, of shades and hue.
Through the unknown, we find our way,
In seeking what the heart may say.

The Art of Losing Oneself

To lose oneself is to be found,
In silent depths where peace is bound.
In quiet moments, let go the fight,
And drift away into the night.

Release the chains of thought and fear,
Embrace the wild, the whisper near.
In solitude, the soul takes flight,
To dance among the stars so bright.

Each heartbeat sings a gentle tune,
A melody beneath the moon.
In surrender, we learn to grow,
The art of losing leads to flow.

With every sunset, let go again,
In loss, we find that we remain.
The journey flows, a ceaseless light,
In artful loss, we find our might.

Waves of a Restless Heart

The ocean calls with a distant sigh,
Restless waves under a cloudy sky.
A heartbeat echoes with every crest,
Yearning for calm, a moment of rest.

Tides pull heartstrings, an ebb and flow,
Secrets hidden, deep down below.
In silence, whispers of dreams untold,
A story of love, in waves, unfolds.

Each crash a promise, each foam a dream,
A dance of emotions, a shimmering beam.
Restless and free, my spirit takes flight,
In the rhythm of waves, I find my light.

As the sun sets low, colors ignite,
Hope rises anew in the pale moonlight.
Forever I chase what the sea has to part,
Lost but alive in the waves of my heart.

Illuminated by the Chase

Under the stars, shadows start to play,
Chasing visions that dance and sway.
With every breath, the thrill ignites,
A journey unfolds under endless nights.

Footsteps echo on this winding road,
Fueled by dreams, I lift the load.
In the chase, I find my grace,
Every turn reveals a new embrace.

The heart races with a fervent beat,
Success a glimpse, oh so sweet.
As dawn breaks forth and shadows wane,
Hope, like sunlight, washes away the pain.

Illumined bright, I stride with might,
In the chase, the world feels right.
The journey's the treasure, the moments we make,
In pursuit of dreams, my spirit won't break.

Fiery Ambitions

In the quiet depths, a spark ignites,
Fiery ambitions set hearts alight.
With every challenge, we rise and push,
Turning dreams from whispers to a fervent hush.

Through trials faced and mountains climbed,
We forge ahead, our spirits primed.
With passion as fuel, we carve our name,
In the book of life, we stoke the flame.

Dancing with doubts, through storms we steer,
Strength lies in the courage to face our fear.
As brands of fire burn in our souls,
We chase our visions, fulfilling our roles.

The world is vast, our dreams take flight,
Boundless ambition, a captivating sight.
In every heartbeat, the fire will stay,
Guiding us forth on this burning way.

Chasing the Dream

In the still of night, with stars so bright,
I chase the dream, my heart in flight.
Every step forward shines with hope,
With every heartbeat, I learn to cope.

Through valleys low and mountains high,
The dream whispers softly, never shy.
Guided by visions of what could be,
Each moment unfolds, a tapestry.

With courage in hand, I greet each dawn,
A journey unwinds from dusk till morn.
Every challenge embraced, I grow,
Chasing the dream, I find my glow.

Let the winds guide me, let the rivers flow,
With every pursuit, my spirit will grow.
Bound to my dreams, I'll boldly soar,
In chasing the dream, I'm forevermore.

The Since of Longing

Beneath the stars, whispers call,
Echoes of love, that rise and fall.
Hearts entwined in shadows cast,
Yearning for a future vast.

Time drips slowly, a river wide,
In silent depths, our dreams reside.
Tracing paths where hopes align,
In the dusk, your hand in mine.

Winds of change, they softly blow,
Stirring feelings we both know.
Each breath a promise, tender and true,
In the heart's silence, I long for you.

Finally, stars align above,
Illuminated by the light of love.
In the quiet, our spirits sing,
Bound forever, come what may bring.

The Art of the Relentless

With every step, the fire grows,
In the face of doubt, it boldly shows.
A dream that's carved in night and day,
With relentless heart, I find my way.

Through the storms and endless rain,
Resilience blooms despite the pain.
Each setback, just a step to climb,
In this dance, I find my rhyme.

Eyes fixed high on distant stars,
Worn-out hands, yet strong with scars.
The art of fighting, brave and bold,
In every story yet untold.

Victory whispers, sweet and low,
In the journey, wisdom flows.
With passion's fire, I chase the light,
For relentless hearts shall win the fight.

The Journey Beyond the Horizon

Beneath the vast and endless sky,
A call to venture, wings to fly.
With each new dawn, horizons shift,
A world of wonders, a radiant gift.

Mountains rise with tales to weave,
Through valleys deep, where dreams believe.
Footprints marked on ancient trails,
In whispers, destiny unveils.

The ocean's roar, a siren's song,
Guiding hearts where they belong.
With courage held in steadfast grace,
Together, we shall find our place.

So hand in hand, let's boldly tread,
On this journey where souls are led.
Beyond the horizon, love awaits,
Each step we take, our spirit creates.

Radiance of the Dream

In twilight's glow, visions bloom,
Casting shadows that dance and loom.
A canvas painted with hopes so bright,
Guided by the softest light.

Dreams emerge like stars in night,
Filling hearts with pure delight.
Each heartbeat sings of battles won,
In the warmth of the rising sun.

Radiance glimmers, whispers clear,
A promise held when you are near.
With open arms, embrace the glow,
In every moment, let love flow.

So chase the visions, let them soar,
For in the dream, we find much more.
Together, let our spirits gleam,
In the endless radiance of the dream.

Through the Veil of Desire

Whispers softly call to me,
Tangled dreams in moonlit glee.
Shadows blend with gentle sighs,
Veils of longing fill the skies.

Fingers brush like fleeting time,
Searching for a rhythm's rhyme.
In the dark, our secrets dwell,
Each heartbeat casts a magic spell.

A longing glance, a stolen kiss,
Moments wrapped in sweet abyss.
Through the mist, our souls entwine,
In the silence, love divine.

Echoes dance in twilight's hush,
Yearning souls collide and rush.
Through the veil, our spirits soar,
In this place, we crave for more.

Burning Bright in Shadows

From deep within, a flame alights,
A beacon found in endless nights.
Though shadows loom and darkness plays,
We burn with fierce, unwavering rays.

In whispered winds, our voices rise,
Casting hope against the skies.
Each flicker fights the creeping chill,
Together strong, we climb the hill.

Embers dance in twilight's haze,
Guiding us through the smoky maze.
With each step, the shadows wane,
In our hearts, a bright refrain.

Burning flames of trust and grace,
In every look, we find our place.
Together forged from ash and fire,
In our bond, we spark desire.

The Dance of Eager Hearts

Underneath the starlit glow,
Two souls waltz with gentle flow.
Every step a soft caress,
In rhythm sweet, we find our press.

With laughter bright, we spin around,
In the silence, love is found.
Time dissolves with every sway,
In this dance, we drift away.

Hands entwined like ivy strong,
In this moment, we belong.
Eyes like candles softly gleam,
In this dance, we chase a dream.

As daybreak nears, we hold on tight,
Every heartbeat, pure delight.
In our dance, forever starts,
Two eager souls and open hearts.

Unfolding Secrets of the Soul

In the stillness, whispers grow,
Secrets shared in twilight's glow.
With each layer, truth revealed,
In the silence, scars are healed.

Gentle words like softest rain,
Wash away the hidden pain.
In the quiet, just we two,
Unfolding dreams both bold and true.

Each heartbeat brings a new design,
Patterns woven, yours and mine.
Through the depths, together we roam,
Finding light to bring us home.

In the dance of trust we weave,
Every moment we believe.
With open hearts and patient grace,
Unfolding secrets, we embrace.

Threads of Ecstasy and Dream

In whispers soft, we weave our fate,
With golden threads of love innate.
Through twilight's glow, our hopes take flight,
In dance of shadows, pure delight.

Moments stitched in vibrant hue,
Bound by dreams that feel so true.
Each heartbeat echoes, sweet and clear,
In fabric bold, we conquer fear.

As stars align in cosmic grace,
We find our magic in this space.
In ecstasy, our spirits soar,
Bound forever, forevermore.

With every thread, a story told,
In love's embrace, we brave the cold.
Together here, our souls will gleam,
In threads of ecstasy and dream.

Echoes of a Hidden Journey

In forests deep where silence reigns,
A path unfolds through gentle plains.
With eyes wide open, hearts unbound,
We seek the truth in whispers found.

Beneath the boughs of ancient trees,
We hear the songs of distant seas.
Each step we take, a tale revived,
In echoes lost, our souls arrived.

The stars above, our guiding light,
Illuminate the shades of night.
With every breath, a promise made,
To walk this road, unafraid.

Through valleys low and mountains high,
We chase the dreams that match the sky.
In hidden journeys, we explore,
The echoes call us to seek more.

Flare of Unbridled Spirit

In feral winds, our spirits dance,
With every heartbeat, we take a chance.
A flare ignites, the night ablaze,
In wild abandon, we lose our gaze.

Unchained and free, we rise above,
With courage fueled by endless love.
Through stormy skies, we find our way,
In vibrant hues, we seize the day.

Each laugh, a spark that lights our soul,
In harmony, we feel the whole.
With hands held tight, we brave the fight,
In fervent dreams, we claim our right.

Flare of spirit, fierce and bold,
Together we can break the mold.
Ignite the fire that dwells within,
In unbridled joy, let life begin.

Roads Under Twilight Skies

As daylight fades, the night awakes,
We wander paths that fate remakes.
With stars above, our journey glows,
In whispered winds, the magic flows.

Through dusky hues, our spirits roam,
On winding roads that call us home.
Each step a story, rich and true,
As twilight wraps its arms around you.

In quiet moments, dreams take flight,
Beneath the canvas of the night.
With every turn, new wonders greet,
In stillness, we find the heartbeat.

Together here, we forge our way,
Under the sky where shadows play.
In twilight's embrace, we rise and thrive,
On roads where magic comes alive.

The Call of the Intrepid

Upon the cliffs where eagles soar,
Adventurers hear the ocean's roar.
With hearts ablaze, they heed the call,
To push their limits, dare to fall.

Through swirling mists and ancient trees,
They chase the winds, they ride the breeze.
With every step, their spirits rise,
In search of truth beneath the skies.

They forge ahead, with dreams in sight,
Bound by the stars, ignited by light.
Each heartbeat echoes, loud and free,
The call of those who dare to be.

So here they stand, on fate's own brink,
With courage found in every wink.
The intrepid shout, in voices wide,
Their journey fuels the fire inside.

Chasing Shadows of Desire

In twilight's glow, the shadows creep,
Desires whisper, promises to keep.
With footsteps quiet, hearts aflame,
They navigate this secret game.

Each glimmer hints at passions stored,
With every sigh, they feel restored.
Through tangled dreams, they twist and twine,
As echoes dance along the line.

The chase is sweet, a fleeting brush,
In every heartbeat, there’s a rush.
Though shadows flicker, lightly cast,
They yearn for moments meant to last.

And in the dark, the dreams align,
As souls connect, both yours and mine.
We chase the stars where hopes conspire,
In endless night, we chase desire.

The Fire that Drives Us

Beneath the surface, embers glow,
A hunger deep, we yearn to know.
With every spark, we feel the heat,
The fire that drives us leads our feet.

Through trials fierce and tempests wild,
We tread the path, though often riled.
With burning hearts and eyes aglow,
We rise again, refuse to slow.

From blinding sires to gentle gleams,
We chase our wild and fevered dreams.
With every step, the flames ignite,
Our spirits soar, our future bright.

Together bound, we fan the flame,
In unity, we stake our claim.
For in the fire, our souls align,
A warrior's heart, forever shine.

Reveling in the Chase

In fields of gold, we run with glee,
With laughter loud and hearts so free.
Each moment shines just like the sun,
In every step, the world's undone.

Through winding trails, sweet secrets lie,
With whispers soft, like breezes sigh.
We dance with fate, we leap with grace,
With every turn, we embrace the chase.

The thrill of life, it fuels our fire,
With every glance, we lift higher.
In this wild ride, we lose the time,
As rhythms pulse, our spirits climb.

So here we are, in blissful flight,
Finding joy in day and night.
Together we rejoice in bliss,
Reveling in each fleeting kiss.

In the Wake of Aspirations

A whisper of dawn breaks the night,
Hope dances in golden light.
Each heart beats with fervent dreams,
Flowing like rivers in silver streams.

Mountains loom with shadows cast,
Yet courage blooms, steadfast.
Every step a chance to rise,
Underneath the vast, bright skies.

Voices echo through the haze,
Guiding paths with fiery blaze.
In the wake of every quest,
The spirit finds its perfect rest.

Beneath the Surface of Yearning

In quiet depths, desires dwell,
A hidden world, a silent swell.
Embers flicker, softly glow,
Beneath the waves of want and woe.

Thoughts like currents, ebb and flow,
Pulling hearts where dreams may go.
Waves crash gently on the shore,
Longing whispers, forevermore.

Eyes cast down at what’s concealed,
Fleeting glimpses, softly revealed.
Each wish a seed, time can nurture,
Growing strong, like a wild suture.

Transcendence of Dreams

In twilight's glow, spirits soar,
Beyond the limits, we explore.
With each heartbeat, visions rise,
Transcendence found in starlit skies.

Every glance a spark ignites,
Crafting worlds of boundless heights.
Imagination takes its flight,
Chasing shadows into the night.

Whispers call from realms unknown,
Where seeds of greatness have been sown.
With courage, we embrace our fate,
In dreams, we shape our own estate.

The Alchemy of Desire

Collecting stardust, we ignite,
Crafting passion in the night.
With every heartbeat, flames arise,
Transforming life with whispered sighs.

Potions brewed in secret space,
Love's elixir, a warm embrace.
Elemental forces blend,
Turning moments into gold, my friend.

In the forge of longing's heat,
We find the strength to stand, repeat.
Alchemy of dreams, divine,
A treasure trove of hearts entwined.

Fireflies of Ambition

In the twilight glow they dance,
Whispers of dreams in each flicker,
Chasing the stars with fearless hearts,
Fueling the fire, growing quicker.

Guided by hope, they light the night,
Eager to reach the moonlit sky,
Every spark a story untold,
In the vastness, their spirits fly.

Through struggles fierce and battles grand,
Their glow refuses to wane or fade,
A testament to the brave who try,
In the darkness, their journeys made.

Chase your fireflies, hold them tight,
For in their shine, the future gleams,
With every step, let passion blaze,
In the realm of hopeful dreams.

The Voyage of the Eager

Set sail on seas of unknown,
With winds of change, they glide with grace,
Hearts full of courage, spirits free,
Charting their course to a brighter place.

The horizon calls with a song so sweet,
Each wave a promise, each swell a chance,
Adventurers bold, they ride the tide,
In the dance of fate, they spin and prance.

Through storms that roar and skies so gray,
They find their strength, their sails held high,
For every setback just fuels the fire,
In the depths of struggle, they learn to fly.

A journey shared, with laughter and tears,
Each moment woven, a tapestry wide,
Together they roam, unbound and true,
On the voyage of the eager, side by side.

A Thrill to Remember

In the whisper of dawn, excitement stirs,
Moments alive with a vibrant chase,
Feeling the rush from the depths of the heart,
Every heartbeat in this blissful space.

Laughter erupts like a fountain of joy,
Dancing on edges, they leap and they soar,
With each thrilling twist, a world unfolds,
Adventure awaits beyond every door.

Memories crafted in bursts of delight,
Savoring flavors of life raw and true,
Caught in the whirlwind of joy unrestrained,
A thrill to remember, like morning dew.

As shadows grow long and the sun bows low,
They gather the pieces of joy in their hands,
Cherish the moments that spark the soul,
In this dance of life, where magic expands.

Splendor in the Seeking

In the heart of the quest, there's a splendor found,
Each step a rhythm, a melody clear,
With eyes wide open, they venture forth,
Seeking the treasures that beckon near.

Mountains high and valleys deep,
Their spirit unyielding, a fire inside,
Every challenge faced, a gem revealed,
In the tapestry of dreams, they abide.

With questions echoing through the night,
Stars overhead like lanterns bright,
For every seeker's journey unfolds,
A story of wonder, a path of light.

In the splendor of seeking, they'll find their way,
A dance of discovery, the world their stage,
With open hearts and curious minds,
They savor the journey, embrace every page.

Kindling the Spirit

In the quiet dawn, dreams arise,
Flickering whispers in the skies.
A spark ignites, a gentle flame,
Nurtured softly, calling your name.

Moments of hope dance in the light,
Transforming shadows into bright.
With every breath, potential glows,
A heart awakened, music flows.

Embers glow with vibrant grace,
In every challenge, find your place.
The courage found within the pain,
Will lift you high, break every chain.

Kindled spirits rise to soar,
Embracing dreams forevermore.
The journey starts with just one spark,
Illuminate the endless dark.

Flight of the Imagination

Lifted high on feathered dreams,
Wings spread wide, or so it seems.
A world painted in colors bright,
Where thoughts take flight into the night.

Clouds become a canvas vast,
Chasing visions, shadows cast.
Creativity, a river flows,
A boundless journey that only grows.

Through the stars and distant lands,
Mysteries await our willing hands.
With every heartbeat, freedom sings,
Uncharted realms, embrace your wings.

In the whirl of infinite space,
Imagination finds its place.
With dreams that soar like the wind,
The heart's true voice is where we begin.

Colors of Eagerness

In a meadow of tender hues,
Life awakens with morning dews.
Each tone a promise, fresh and new,
Colors of eagerness in view.

Joyful reds and calming blues,
Yellows bright as the sun breaks through.
A palette rich with every shade,
Inviting hearts to unafraid.

Brush strokes paint a vibrant scene,
Every hue tells what could have been.
In this beauty, dreams take form,
A symphony of life, the norm.

With open arms, embrace the day,
Let eagerness guide your way.
Through colors bright, let courage bloom,
In every heart, belief finds room.

The Energy of Belief

A pulse ignites with every thought,
In the depths of hope, we are caught.
Faith like roots stretches wide and deep,
Nurturing dreams that we keep.

Whispers of strength in the night,
A torchbearer's glow, pure and bright.
Every heartbeat fuels the fire,
A symphony of the heart's desire.

With every trial, rise and stand,
Belief empowers, gives us command.
In the realm where courage lives,
The energy of belief truly gives.

So when the clouds of doubt surround,
Trust the power that can be found.
For with each step taken in faith,
We weave our dreams, create our wraith.

Heartstrings Tethered to Tomorrow

In twilight's glow, we dare to dream,
With whispers soft, hopes gently beam.
A thread of fate, a pull divine,
We chase the stars, their paths entwine.

Each heartbeat sings of future days,
Where love's embrace ignites the blaze.
Together we rise, hand in hand,
In a world that sparkles, vast and grand.

Across the shores of time we sail,
With courage fierce, we will not fail.
Through trials fierce and tempests strong,
Our hearts will weave a timeless song.

So take my hand, let's dance through night,
With every step, we ignite the light.
For heartstrings tied to tomorrows bright,
Lead us onward, taking flight.

Limbs Touched by Inspiration

In gentle winds, the branches sway,
A dance of leaves, in bright array.
The sun breaks through with warming grace,
While shadows play, they find their place.

With every step, the earth does hum,
A melody, soft and yet so dumb.
As nature whispers all around,
Our souls are stirred, in beauty found.

From mountain peaks to valleys low,
Inspiration flows, a steady flow.
With every breath, we feel alive,
Limbs touched by dreams, we begin to rise.

So follow paths where shadows lead,
Let curiosity plant the seed.
For in each moment, a spark ignites,
And limbs touched with wonder take flight.

The Quest for Boundless Joy

In fields of gold, our laughter rings,
We chase the light that freedom brings.
With every step, we break the mold,
In search of treasures, bright and bold.

Where worries fade, and troubles part,
We gather moments, purest art.
Each smile exchanged, a thread of grace,
A joyous dance in time and space.

Through valleys deep and mountains high,
We seek the dreams, we dare to fly.
With open hearts, we pave the way,
In quest of joy, we'll never sway.

When shadows fall, and spirits wane,
Together we rise, through joy and pain.
For in our hearts, the spark remains,
The quest for joy, forever reigns.

Labyrinth of Aspired Moments

In winding paths where dreams entwine,
We wander lost, yet feel the sign.
Each turn reveals a brand new face,
Within the maze, we find our place.

With echoes soft, the past will call,
Reminding us we've lived through all.
In every step, the lessons learned,
Through trials faced, our spirits burned.

So onward now, through shadows cast,
We weave through time, embrace the vast.
For in this labyrinth, we shall find,
A tapestry of heart and mind.

And when the light begins to fade,
We hold the moments, unafraid.
In the labyrinth, love's gentle trace,
Guides us home to our rightful space.

Pursuing the Unchained

In the whispers of the night,
Dreams take flight, unconfined.
Hearts in rhythm with the stars,
Freedom sings from afar.

Chasing shadows, we ignite,
Passions burn, a fierce light.
With every step, we defy,
Boundless souls that touch the sky.

Paths untraveled, voices clear,
We embrace what we hold dear.
Together, we break the mold,
Stories of the brave unfold.

In the journey, we are one,
Beneath the moon, 'til the sun.
Through the storms, we find our way,
Unchained spirits, bold and gay.

Harmonies of Hustle

In the city's pulse, we strive,
Dreamers dance, our hopes alive.
Rhythms blend in every street,
Life's a song, a steady beat.

With every dawn, we rise anew,
Fueling fire, the work we do.
Voices join, a vibrant choir,
Crafting futures, lifting higher.

Late nights filled with fervent dreams,
Unity flows in all our schemes.
Brick by brick, we build our fate,
In the hustle, we create.

Every challenge, a chance to learn,
In the chaos, passions burn.
Together, we face what's true,
Harmonies born from me and you.

The Veil of Inspiration

Softly draped in threads of gold,
Whispers of the brave, retold.
A spark ignites, a guiding light,
In shadows deep, we find our might.

Lifting veils to see the dream,
In the silence, thoughts redeem.
Glimmers dance in every heart,
Inspiration, a timeless art.

Cast your doubts and fears away,
In the light, let passion sway.
Through the fog, the vision clear,
In every pulse, our purpose near.

With open wings, we rise and soar,
On the winds of hope, we explore.
Together, we reach for the stars,
Embracing life, with all its scars.

Fervor Unleashed

Within our hearts, a roaring flame,
Fervor blooms, we stake our claim.
With each breath, ambition grows,
In the depths, our courage glows.

We rise to meet the stormy skies,
In every challenge, strength relies.
Voices loud, a fierce refrain,
Together, we break every chain.

Hearts ablaze with dreams in sight,
Marching forth, we seize the light.
In the struggle, we find peace,
A fervent bond that will not cease.

Through the trials, dreams take flight,
In our unity, the world ignites.
Passion guides, our spirits free,
Fervor unleashed, eternally.

The Quest of the Soul

In the twilight of thought, we seek,
The whispers of heart, soft and meek.
Through shadows and light, we wander wide,
Finding the truth where hopes reside.

Each step a story, each breath a song,
In the silence of night, we feel we belong.
With courage as guide, and love as our map,
We journey through worlds, in an endless lap.

Deep in the stillness, we often find,
Fragments of dreams that once intertwined.
Like stars in the dark, they flicker and glow,
Illuminating paths we yearn to follow.

At the end of the quest, what treasures await?
A mirror of souls, a truth that's innate.
In every heart is a quest, fierce and bright,
The essence of being, our eternal light.

Infinite Aspirations

With each rising dawn, new dreams unfurl,
In the dance of the cosmos, our spirits twirl.
Beyond the horizon, possibilities soar,
Infinite aspirations, forever we explore.

Like mountains and rivers, our goals intertwine,
Every heartbeat whispers, 'You're destined to shine.'
The canvas of life, painted bold and bright,
In colors of hope, we chase the light.

With whispering winds that carry our flame,
Each step we take, we're never the same.
Through valleys of doubt and peaks of delight,
We hold our ambitions, steadfast in sight.

United in vision, as stars in the night,
Together we rise, igniting the flight.
For every desire ignites a new chance,
In the rhythm of dreams, let's continue to dance.

Dreams Set Aglow

In the still of the night, our dreams take flight,
Painting the dark with a soft, silver light.
Whispers of wishes, both tender and grand,
Illuminate visions by destiny's hand.

With each gentle sigh, a vision unfolds,
Stories of hope, in the night air told.
Like fireworks bursting in colorful streams,
The skies come alive with our wildest dreams.

Through valleys of shadows and mountains of grace,
We chase our own truths, finding our place.
With hearts set aglow, we rise and we soar,
Boundless ambitions, forever explore.

In the canvas of stars, our futures align,
Each glimmer a promise, a spark, a sign.
Embrace the unknown, let inspiration flow,
For life is a journey, where dreams set aglow.

Radiant Pursuits

In the warmth of the dawn, we chase what's true,
Radiant pursuits in skies vast and blue.
With passion ignited, each heart finds its way,
Through trials and triumphs, we seize the day.

Like rivers flowing, our paths intertwine,
Carving the landscape where dreams brightly shine.
Each moment a jewel, a treasure to hold,
In the tapestry woven, our stories unfold.

With laughter as music and love as our guide,
In radiant pursuits, we take every stride.
For life's an adventure, an exquisite dance,
A symphony played in the heart's expanse.

Together we rise, in the sun's warm embrace,
In the glow of our dreams, we find our place.
In pursuit of the light, we shall not be swayed,
For in our hearts' journey, our legacy's made.

The Pulse of Obsession

In shadows deep where whispers dwell,
A heart is bound, a secret spell.
Desire ignites a fervent flame,
In every thought, you call my name.

Contorted paths we choose to tread,
Chasing ghosts that fill our head.
Each breath a tether, a binding thread,
In this madness, love is bred.

An endless dance in twilight's glow,
With every step, the tempo grows.
Echoes linger, fervent and wild,
In obsession's grip, I am your child.

When daylight breaks, will you be near?
Or will the shadows reappear?
This pulse of us, relentless beat,
A cycle trapped, yet bittersweet.

A Tapestry of Hopes

Threads entwined in colors bold,
Crafting stories yet untold.
Each stitch a dream, a whispered prayer,
In the fabric of the air.

Woven wonders of laughter bright,
Glimmers of love in the fading light.
Every heartbeat, a vibrant hue,
We gather hopes, forever new.

Beneath the stars, our wishes soar,
Spanning realms, like waves on shore.
A tapestry, both rich and rare,
Woven with kindness, spun with care.

In every thread, a journey shared,
In joys and sorrows, deeply bared.
Together we rise, come what may,
A tapestry of hopes, come what may.

Echoes of a Dreamer

In twilight's hush, the whispers call,
A dreamer's heart will never fall.
Through ancient woods and starlit skies,
Imagination takes to rise.

Echoes of laughter, songs of old,
In every shadow, stories told.
Beneath the moon, where silence reigns,
The dreamer finds what life contains.

In visions bright, the world expands,
With every thought, a thousand strands.
A journey carved in midnight's gleam,
Awakening the deepest dream.

So take my hand, let's drift away,
Chasing dreams that dare to play.
In echoes soft, we'll find our way,
A dreamer's heart holds endless sway.

Flames of Creation

In every spark, a vision born,
From ashes gray, the new is sworn.
Fires dance with fervent grace,
Igniting passion in this place.

We mold our thoughts like molten glass,
In the crucible where shadows pass.
With every stroke, the canvas sings,
The flames of creation, brightening things.

Chasing embers through the night,
Crafting dreams in the fading light.
In flickering flames, our spirits soar,
Through trials faced, we'll brave the storm.

So let the fire burn and glow,
In every heart a flame will grow.
From seeds of thought, we'll cultivate,
The flames of creation, sealing fate.

Printed in the USA
CPSIA information can be obtained
at www.ICGtesting.com
LVHW020857171024
794056LV00002B/580

9 789916 880456